Make the Right Move

The Answers to 30 questions you need to know to Maximize your Real Estate Dollar

JOHN RICE

DEDICATION

To my brilliant and beautiful wife. Your passion for knowledge and relentless quest for improvement within ourselves inspires me and shows me every day how my love for you can grow with no bounds. Thank you!

To my most amazing daughter. Your zest for life and living in the moment is a constant joy. You are a true example for others to follow and show me each day what God had in mind when he placed us on this earth.

To my wonderful clients. Without you my passion for real estate would be only partially fulfilled. Thank you for placing your faith and trust in me and allowing me to continue to assist you.

CONTENTS

PROLOGUE

- *What is the first step to buying a home in today's market?*
- *I've never SOLD before – how to I begin?*

This book will answer these and other questions. It is designed to review commonly asked questions about the home buying process.

Each home, each property, each person is unique and yet over the years many properties and many people have asked very similar questions. It is my intent to share with you thoughts on these most commonly asked questions to give you a jump start on your success in your next move.

CHAPTER 1:

WHY YOU NEED THIS BOOK

For many, your home is your biggest asset. As with anything in life, there are many ways to get things done. Doesn't it make sense that when dealing with "your biggest asset" you make as few mistakes as possible? And there it is – the reason this book exists: educate, inform, inspire.

As a homeowner in today's market, you recognize the joy of owning. Yes, there is ongoing maintenance but there is something that no words can describe – the place to call "home." When your present space no longer suits your needs, it's time to move on. Will you get every dollar out of your home the market will bear? Will you look back in hindsight and recognize the "Woulda-coulda-shoulda's" that add up to tens of thousands of dollars? Or will you maximize your real estate experience and apply the knowledge in these chapters to set yourself up for success?

As a buyer entering today's market, the world is full of exciting opportunities. Never before has so much information been available to you as a consumer. How will you filter, process, and apply this information? Are you aware of the opportunities that currently exist? What questions should be asked to produce the answers you need to maximize your real estate purchase experience?

Real estate has made more millionaires than any other investment. Now you might not desire to be a millionaire or even billionaire. But one thing is for sure, follow the right plan, at the right time, crafted by those with experience, and you will have the greatest likelihood of success.

For me, real estate is a passion. Helping people find a home they love, and achieving their real estate dreams fuels me. Throughout these chapters, I share thoughts about how you can truly make the most of your real estate experience. I sincerely wish you the best in your real estate quest and look forward to meeting you in person some day!

CHAPTER 2:

WHAT STEPS SHOULD I EXPECT FOR PURCHASING A HOME?

Buying a home can be fun and exciting! When it's done right, the reward is superb. The first and most important step is understanding the simple process. Here's the outline of the Home Buying 8 Step Process with us:

1. Consultation: Where we discuss what type of home you want, where you want it, and your price range.

Often as home buyers you have many questions. Scheduling time to sit down and talk about your housing needs, what you are looking for in a home, and review items to consider. You also want to ensure a comfortable budget is set.

Next we recommend getting a pre-approval letter from a lender of your choice. This step helps you when you bring an offer to a seller. If you would like recommendations, we'd be glad to assist you in finding a mortgage officer who can meet your needs.

2. As your buyers agent, we educate you, and we tour homes until we find you your new home.

In step one, we outlined a lot of the factors that are important to you, now its time to go see them in person. Items to consider here are neighborhoods, home style, and proximity to things that are important to you. We help you think about all of these things.

3. The comprehensive market analysis is done to determine the best bid for the home of your choice.

Once you've found a home that you think has enough of what you want (remember no home is "perfect"). We will help you determine the right amount to offer. Some items in determining this are what the owner paid for the home, taxes, and the prices of other sold homes in the area.

4. We write the offer together – we thoroughly review each step so you know everything we are writing.

Offers can be written to be contingent on:

- The buyer obtaining financing

- Having the property inspected by a professional inspector within ten days of an accepted offer

- Additional items as deemed necessary

5. Offer is presented, and negotiations begin.

After writing an offer with your interest in mind, we present the offer to the seller and their agent (if an agent represents a seller). At this point, we might negotiate back and forth until all parties agree on price and terms. Once all parties agree on the price and terms an earnest deposit is collected to hold the property in your name. The earnest deposit will vary based on the home's price. Typically, an amount equal to 1%-2% is best but sometimes $500 is enough and other times much more is best. Plan on 1% and the situation will tell us if we need to adjust to anything else.

6. Inspections are held at the home. If any items need attention, these items are brought before the seller to be fixed.

During the inspection process, you hire a home inspector to come and inspect the home. The buyer typically pays the cost of the inspection, because it's for your protection. The home inspector is there on your behalf to apply their knowledge to your potential purchase. They will inspect the entire structure. The inspection includes: the inside and outside of the home from top to bottom. They examine the basement and foundation. Often there will be items that remain with the home, appliances and such, these will be tested to verify they are in working order. The inspection includes electrical and plumbing systems, the roof and more – it's a very thorough inspection. Plus, you can elect for additional typical inspections like a termite inspection or a radon gas inspection. In Michigan I recommend both of these be done, but it's your choice as a buyer. A termite inspection is required if you are purchasing through FHA and some other government back loans.

The typical cost for an inspector is about $350-$400 not including termite and radon inspections (usually about $125-150 each.) Each inspector has their set of fees and may charge more if the home is much larger than average (typically about 1800 sq ft or less.)

If there is a well or septic system involved, we will typically recommend having the well, and septic system inspected. In some counties this is required. It is also a good practice to ensure the tanks have been pumped within the last two years. It is typically a seller expense, and usually their agent has already prompted them to be prepared for this to come up. Regardless we write the offer to protect you here as well.

If anything comes up during the inspection that is an issue, we can negotiate this with the seller. Almost every home has something that is broken or needs some level of repair, even if it's incredibly little. You may decide not to take any action about correcting an issue. An inspector will point out recommendations that while important may lean more toward personal preference than having to be fixed. It will be your decision. Other times issues arise that may need attention prior to proceeding, this is when we talk about our options and renegotiate with the seller.

Most sellers have done their best to maintain the home in as good of condition as possible. Sometimes, though, things get overlooked, and when the inspector brings it to everyone's attention, the seller is willing to correct it.

We proceed, once you are satisfied with the corrections to any potential issues.

7. The mortgage people begin to process the loan, and we prepare for closing.

At this point, we have passed inspections, and we've let your mortgage representative know. At this point, the mortgage company will order the appraisal (a third party who helps the bank determine the value of the property you are purchasing.) Just like we helped you determine an offering price and walked you through a market analysis of the home, the bank hires an appraiser to do their "market analysis." Once the property has been determined to be valued "equal to" or "greater than" your mortgage amount, they will proceed. Typically, appraisals will run around $350; sometimes less, sometimes, more. Some lenders/banks will pay for the appraisal out of their "application fee." It just depends on the bank/lender you choose.

At this point, we are usually within 2.5 to 3.5 weeks of closing on your home. Sometimes FHA loans can take longer (about 45 days from the date we settle on an agreement with the seller.)

8. The closing: Congratulations you have just completed the Home Buying 8 Step Process to owning your new home!

Here we are! You're sitting at the closing table signing all the documents everyone has told you about.....and we're sitting here with you. Yes, we come to the closing – we're here for every step of your home purchase. So what happens here? First off: we're at a title agency. Title agencies act as an independent third party that oversees the transaction and records your property with the county and city where your home is.

By now, you've already viewed the bulk of all the documents you're signing either through us in the purchase agreement or with your lender. Prior to sitting here at the table, we've reviewed together the closing statement (otherwise known as the HUD or HUD-1 statement) which has all the final financials on it. This statement tells us to the penny, where your purchase dollars are going, including the cash you need to bring to close. This final amount is typically provided 24-48 hours prior to close (it depends on the lender and the closing office coordinating the delivery of your documents and their preparation.) You will need to bring the final amount in the form of a cashier check made out to the name of the closing office, along with your driver's license. If you are purchasing the home in more than one name (as a couple, co-signer, or another type of relationship), you will each need to be present and bring your driver's license.

Typically, by this date, the utility companies have been contacted to ensure you're going to have electric and gas turned on, for when you take possession of the home. At the closing table, you receive the keys – unless you've allowed the seller to stay a few extra days to pack their things after the close.

After all the documents have been signed by both you and the seller (typically about 1 hour total.) your closing is done! You are now the proud new owner of your home!

Congratulations!

To learn more and take advantage of the bonus material head over to buyers.johnricerealtor.com

CHAPTER 3:

STEPS TO SELLING YOUR HOME

As a seller, often your main objective is to sell your home for the highest dollar value considering the time frame in which you need to sell.

The first step to considering your properties value is an "on-site review." A tour of your property understanding what makes it unique, what sets it apart, and what are possible improvements that should be addressed to maximize its selling price?

Step 1: On-Site Review: What does an on-site review look like to the seller? You as the seller will give us a tour of your home to show what you like about the home/house and also what you dislike. This tour of the whole of the home will give us the information to provide you the right price. After conducting the on-site review, one of the two scenarios will happen:

1. There will have been enough other similar homes to offer pricing and time on the market projections immediately

2. A follow-up appointment will be set to discuss specific listing price and time on the market projections – allowing time to determine the best case scenario for your property.

Step 2: Marketing Time: Next begins the marketing of the property. Factoring in your home's style, uniqueness, and amenities your marketing plan will be designed to best suited to the ideal audience and most likely buyer for your property.

Step 3: The Offer: There are many factors that come into play during the offer including but not limited to:

- Purchase price - It is important but not the only factor involved in an offer

- Financing vs. Cash? - How is the buyer proposing to pay for the property – where is their proof? Do they need to sell a home before they can buy yours?

- Possession time – How long will you be in the home after close and will you pay a fee? In many cases, you are giving your keys to the buyer at close or near that date.   There are ways to negotiate more time in your home after close and typically for a small daily or monthly "rent" fee. This part of the negotiation is particularly helpful if you are looking to move into a new residence, and you do not have possession of it yet.

- Survey – Does performing a new survey need done at this time and if so who is paying for this?

- Well and Septic health and function - Most health departments require the seller to have the well tested for the safety of its drinking water and the testing of the septic system for proper function and safety. It is typically a seller's responsibility, and most buyer purchase agreements ask the seller to pay for this.

- Title insurance - It is common for most buyers to ask a seller to participate in title insurance, so be prepared to factor this into your total closing costs as a seller.

- Property taxes – You pay taxes typically both in the summer and in the winter. How will those be handled at closing? Typically they are pro-rated to the day of close, but it's a negotiation, so any agreement is possible between both buyer and seller.

- Closing time – When does the buyer want to close? Typically a conventional loan can be closed within 30 -45 days. Other loan types such as FHA or VA maybe 45-60 days. Cash closes can be almost immediate. It all varies, so it is important to hash this out up front.

- Other items - Because each property is unique there are often "other items" that will be part of an offer. It is important to review these other items carefully to ensure what they mean and how they can affect the deal overall.

These and other factors affect your net at closing, the amount you will receive from the sale. Calculating these factors up front BEFORE your home goes on the market is important. Calculating them once an offer has been received is helpful, but the calculations done once an agreed offer is in place, sets you up for success. Understanding the numbers will minimize stress as we move toward closing.

To learn more and obtain the bonus material head over to sellers.johnricerealtor.com

CHAPTER 4:

FIRST TIME HOME BUYERS: WHERE DO YOU START?

Congratulations! You're at a point where you feel it's time to get a place of your own. It's such an exciting time! In fact, recently I worked with Ben and Allison, and they were in a very similar situation. They had spent several years renting, but they knew it was time to go ahead and get a place of their own. When they came to me, the first thing they talked about was -What were the things that they wanted in a house? What were the pros and cons of buying in certain areas? And what were the factors that they knew they couldn't live without in their new home?

It's different for everyone though. For Ben and Allison, it happened to be that they wanted sidewalks, at least three bedrooms and a location close to Ben's work. Those were important factors for them. We took that information, and at the same time, helped match them up with a network of partners we have for mortgages. Our next discussion was on a budget, and helping them to understand what is the best budget for them and their situation. Based on this budget how much will they be able to spend? Then together with the budget, and everything they wanted in their house, we designed a plan to be able to create success for them.

That's why we have the First Time Home Buyer section on the web page. It is designed with tools and resources – with you - in mind, to be able to look at what's out there on the market (http://johnricerealtor.com/first-time-buyers/).

Maybe you already have a rough idea of a budget of what you're looking to spend, and of what you're looking for in your next home, just as Ben and Allison did. Then utilize these pages as a resource, but also, feel free to reach out to me; that is why I'm here. I'm here to help you design and craft a plan for your success in your new home.

Remember your extra bonus material can be found at: buyers.johnricerealtor.com

CHAPTER 5:

WHAT IS A HOT MARKET?

I've been asked that question a lot lately. What is a hot market?

Well, to break it down, it's all about supply and demand. What that means is that demand is high, and supply is down – there are lots of people looking to buy, but not many places to see. It means prices can go up, and things can sell very quickly.

It's very important for:

A. Buyers to be very prepared and understand what they are looking for in a new home.

B. Sellers to understand that their house could sell quickly. Once a home sells, the seller must identify where they're going to be moving.

In a hot market when inventory is low, the more you prepare before you start, the less it is going to seem like a battle.

To checkout the free bonus guide on buying and selling in a Hot Market go to:

buyers.johnricerealtor.com

sellers.johnricerealtor.com

CHAPTER 6:

MOVE UP BUYERS: WHERE DO YOU START?

Congratulations! You're at a point where you're thinking of a larger home. Maybe something has happened in your life where now, it's time. It reminds me of some recent clients I worked with, Tony and Derek. They came to came to me, and when I first met them, they needed to shorten their commute. But their current home presented certain challenges. In their case, it was a historical home that needed to sell for more than the neighborhood was originally going to bear.

19

So, our first step was to sit down and craft a plan. We toured their home, and I had a chance to understand what it is that they love about their home. Now we could begin to transfer that and create the buyer marketplace; who's going to be the buyer of their home? That was step one.

Then we talked about, where are they going to move? If they could paint a picture, what is their next ideal place? When they took that first step into their new home, what did they want to see and feel? Where was the kitchen? How about bedrooms? What type of view was out the windows?

A big thing for them was not only budget, but also location. They knew that they wanted a certain setting and only a certain length of a drive to work. And so, with those factors in mind, we had them consult with a mortgage expert to understand best what that budget needed to look like - what would be comfortable for them.

And then it was my job to get out there and look and see – Ok, what type of houses are out there within their parameters? And this is all before we even put a sign in the yard! Working together to understand what our common goals are going to be, and then we go from there.

Tony and Derek were very open and said, "Ok, now that we know the strategy for our next home, how do we get there?" The question that is being asked is, "How can we work best as a team to achieve our goals?" And that's what this website is all about (http://johnricerealtor.com/move-buyers/). It's designed to help you be successful in your next move.

The resources that are here in this book are designed to help you understand what's out there in the market. On my website at johnricerealtor.com, I have created tools for you to begin your next move. On the website if you have an idea of the budget you're looking to spend already, you can draft the parameters right there, and see if everything that fits in that area. If you know your school district, if you know the location – it's right there. Also to that, if you have a rough idea of how much you'd like to get out of your home, I do have an evaluation tool right there on the page. But just like Tony and Derek utilized me as a resource – that's why I'm here. I'm here to help you achieve your goal. And with that in mind, I encourage you to explore the MOVE UP BUYER section of the website (http://johnricerealtor.com/move-buyers/). Next, contact me, so that I have the opportunity to learn more about what you're looking to achieve, and together, we can help you be successful.

CHAPTER 7:

HOW DO WE GET STARTED?

How do I get started, figure out a budget, and get approved?

The first thing you want to do is start by going to your favorite lending institution (credit union, bank, whatever). Then also go on my website (http://johnricerealtor.com/partners/) and then you'll see the vendors on my partner list I've trusted my clients to for years. These are the loan officers who will be able to help you understand what you need to do, get pre-approved, and establish a budget.

After you've had a chance to meet with a loan officer, you will get the opportunity to establish a monthly budget. Most likely the loan officer will have covered your mortgage payment, your home insurance payment, and your taxes. The next biggest thing you want to consider is utilities – how much will it be to keep the lights on per month? How much will it cost to heat the home? When we go to identify that house that you like, we're going to be able to ask the seller, in most cases, what was their utility payment history?

So we can help you establish a budget, and make sure it's comfortable not only right now, today, but then also on into the future. And that's the whole idea. This whole buying a house thing is a lot of fun, and we can make it comfortable.

Recently in working with Chad and Katie, when we first sat down and understood what it was they were looking to achieve, I learned a few things. First and foremost, they didn't come by their house the way people traditionally would. Many people might have bought it through me directly, or maybe through another agent, at another time before we met. And so, they've had experience with an agent. For Chad and Katie, they had inherited a house – they bought it through the family. So, they had never experienced the real estate transaction – ever.

Everything about their transaction to date was non-traditional. One of the things that we sat down and talked about was, what can you experience over the next weeks and months while your house is on the market? Or maybe better put, what should you expect to experience. That was the first thing we covered.

Then we talked about going through the house, and we all put on what I call the buyer goggles - not beer goggles, but buyer goggles. So Chad, Katie, and I, along with their daughter,– who is only 3 –the four of us walked through the house together. We took a look at everything in the house and said, how is a buyer going to perceive the kitchen? What will they see in the living room? How will they feel walking into a bedroom or the master bedroom?

In doing so, we came up with a brief list of things that easily could change. In the living room, we made a small change to the furniture arrangement. In the master bedroom, some reorganizing was needed which involved taking a few of those seasonal items and placing them in a downstairs closet. It maximized each room for the buyer's perception.

The next thing that we did with Chad and Katie was sit down and talk about their timing. As we got into focusing on their timing, we looked at different ways that different times of the year affect a sale – that is when they might be able to maximize their sales time. For them, it happened to be late spring /early summer because they're in a good school system, and they want to attract a family that wants to move during the summer. So, we talked about what effect that would have on their move. In the end, we sat down, and we talked about – ok, once we have a buyer in place, what can we expect from that point forward?

Once Chad and Katie were comfortable with understanding the process in place, then we knew it was time to move on, and talk about – what is that next house going to look like for them? Again this was so that they can go confidently in that direction.

Get the free guide that Chad and Katie used to get started by going here: buyers.johnricerealtor.com

CHAPTER 8:

HOW DO I KNOW I'M GETTING A GOOD HOME?

The other day when working with Mary and Dave, we came to a house that was perfect for them. Initially, a couple of other houses were high on the list, but in the end, a house out in the country just seemed like the perfect fit for them. So, we decided to look at making an offer.

One of the things the listing agent told us, "So that you know, this house was already inspected by another buyer. Their financing fell through, but the house passed inspection with flying colors."

Ok. So the deal fell apart previously, but not because of inspection supposedly. That's good information. But the question becomes - how much due diligence do you still pursue to ensure that you're getting the right house?

The option was one of two things; do we want to go to the original inspector, and ask to buy that inspection, and take their word for it? Or, do we hire our inspector, somebody who we know, like, and trust and, in this case, somebody I'd used for years. By going down that path, you make sure that the proper due diligence is in place.

In the end, they chose to have a completely independent, new person take a look at the house – and it was a good thing that they did. The original inspector had missed that there was carpenter ant damage, which was not expensive, but important to note. Also, the furnace had a cracked heat exchanger and completely needed to be replaced. It ended up being almost a $4,000 expense to replace the furnace. Because Dave and Mary had paid $500 for the inspection, and we were able to negotiate successfully that the seller take care of the furnace for them - the larger of the two items.

In the end, Dave and Mary felt like they won. And now, they feel comfortable that they are getting a good house, and this boosted their confidence for the rest of the experience.

So often after selecting the home to offer on, the question becomes - "How do I know I'm getting a good home?"

Here are some guidelines my team follows making sure that when the purchase agreement is written you are taken care of and protected:

1. Start off with a lot of due diligence. When looking at houses, we're not just looking for fun; we're looking for function, as well.

2. Make sure we compare this home to others and do a market analysis of the home. Does this line up with the rest of the neighborhood? Is it a good deal? What are you looking to achieve with this house in the next 5, 10, or 20 years? A lot of times your first house isn't your last house, so you want to make sure it's a good value.

3. Something very important to consider is having your home professionally inspected. As Dave and Mary luckily found out, that a professional inspection can save you not only money, but many headaches in the future. Professional home inspectors know and understand the fit and function of a house. They will be able to tell you exactly what this house looks like, and what kind of maintenance you be expecting, and whether there have been things that the seller has neglected. Knowing this, you can go back and either ask the seller about it or just be aware of up front. Frankly, if the repairs or

maintenance are too big and too great for you to take on as a new home owner, you can cancel that contract out, and move on to the next one.

That's one of the best parts of working with a pro, who will make sure that you understand what you're purchasing right up front.

Your bonus material is waiting for you at buyers.johnricerealtor.com

CHAPTER 9:

WHAT IS THE BEST BUYERS STRATEGY IN A HOT MARKET?

One of the things to make sure that your offer stays front and center with a seller in today's market is to think of a strategy that removes as many pain points for a seller as possible.

Some things to consider - in a "hot" or fast moving market, a seller may sell their house very quickly. What does that mean for them now? They might be scared about where they will go next. So that's something to consider and come up with a plan on how to potentially ease that fear.

Secondly there are many ways you can offer to a seller a particular price, but the question is, "Will that price get me this home I want?" One of the ways you can make sure that you maximize your purchase is to consider an offer that blocks all other buyers and puts you in the number one position.

How do you do that?

It is a simple strategy, so let's take a look at it, but also look into the psychology of it for you as the buyer.

Many times as the buyer, you are looking for ways to save money or to make sure that you are getting a deal or want the best value for the money you will be spending. To get you in the number one position, you will need to offer full or maybe sometimes over asking price.

Do you want the house?

Is it located in the school district that you want your children to learn in so that they have the best educational opportunities or extracurricular activities available? Is it centrally located to work, shopping, church, or any other activity in which you participate? Does it have that dream view out the backyard that you have always wanted? If this is "that" house, then paying full price or over is well worth it.

Some other ways that add value to a deal for a seller would be – look at what the seller is offering, beyond the real estate – are they considering including kitchen appliances? Are they considering including the washer and dryer? But beware - if they do not include those, don't ask for them - keep your offer very clean.

Lastly, one of the ways that I've seen a lot of buyers be successful in the low-interest rate environment is to not ask your seller to pay for closing costs on your behalf. Instead, consider paying your closing costs. You could even go to your mortgage loan officer and ask them, "What kind of small interest rate bump would there be to roll my closing costs into my rate?" Sometimes it's only a quarter of a point – which would increase your rate very little - and include closing costs in your interest rate. Use this technique rather than come to the table with 3-4% extra to cover the typical closing costs.

Recently I worked with a new home buyer. She is an under 30 buyer in today's market and was looking to take advantage of the low-interest rates that are out there. She wants to stop renting and get into her first house. She had lived elsewhere in the country – and now she wanted to come back home and be near her mom and dad. It was the perfect environment for her to shop for her new home.

So, we started with a budget, and her budget was ultimately less than what was approved, which I find a lot of buyers prefer. By the time you add in utilities, and taxes and everything else, it's wise that you're not spending to the absolute max approval that a bank has given.

Secondly, we took some time and figured out what it was that she wanted in a home. Originally, she thought, maybe a condo would be perfect. But, in the end, she chose a single family house.

Lastly, Megan had an idea of the area, and she knew the type of house she wanted. She wanted some character in it – so probably not something brand new – but she also didn't want something so big that it would consume her every free moment. We wanted to make sure that her house was a nice size to maintain without too much stress.

We found her the right house, and then it was time to craft the right offer. We sat down and talked about the seller's asking price, and what was the seller's next move. Well, we found out through due diligence that the seller would be moving into another home. Since they were not building, it meant that they would probably need 30-45 days to be able to secure that new house and move in.

So, we wrote that into the offer. Megan wanted to keep her purchase price as low as possible, to save her a few extra dollars. So we factored in possession after closing - how long, and for what amount would the seller stay on the property? In this case, we gave them 30 days free. Additionally, for the sake of negotiations, we wrote in that the seller would leave a washer and dryer, with the idea that they would probably counter us and ask us to keep the washer and dryer. We intentionally wrote that in, so we would have another way to say, seller, go ahead, you can keep that. But, we will need you to keep the purchase price lower.

Our last strategy was we wrote an attractive purchase price that wasn't unreasonable. The offer was high enough that Megan was comfortable, and at the same time, low enough to either do one of two things

A. Illicit an acceptance from the seller, because we had written in all the other terms.

B. Result in a very small counter to make sure that the seller would start and have a conversation with us, and not just blow us off.

In the end, we ended up going back and forth a little bit, and we were able to keep the price low for Megan because of the other written in points. And Megan purchased a great home for herself.

Those are a few small strategies that you can do to help keep that offer front and center to the seller. If you do end up in a competing situation, you put yourself in a high potential for success, for being the winning bidder, when you've removed all the potential pain points for a seller.

Use the bonus material found at buyers.johnricerealtor.com to give you a tactical advantage with your buyer strategy.

CHAPTER 10:

AS A BUYER IN TODAY'S MARKET, WHAT SHOULD I EXPECT?

Buyers- what's going to be the first step to your success in today's real estate market? Well, number one, you need to plan ahead.

Second, don't be afraid to know that you might feel a little behind the eight ball when you first get started.

Why?

Other buyers, who are looking to purchase a home, have already started this process ahead of you. They went through the same pains of feeling like, "Oh my gosh everything is selling before I can look at it."

But, what happens is, once you get a chance to get your stride, you understand what you're looking for in a home. You develop a budget and determine the area where you want to buy. Of course, you work with a good professional. It gets to a point where everything comes together.

Remember that once you have an opportunity to get out and experience a few houses, there are going to be other buyers who go through this house who know it's the right one for them. You might not be at that point yet, today, after touring that first house, but other buyers around you may already know that's the right house for them. Don't be pressured by the market, but do understand that when you do find the right one, it's important to act. In today's market, often, you will be offering very close to list price, or possibly even over list price.

Anytime, such as with today's market where we have fewer homes on the market, and more buyers looking. It creates a demand, and to win in today's market, as a buyer, we need to be aggressive and set you up for the success of purchasing that home you desire.

Lessen any surprises in today's market when you pick up your bonus material at <u>buyers.johnricerealtor.com</u>

CHAPTER 11:

WHAT ABOUT INTEREST RATES?

Often I'm asked by my clients, what is a good interest rate? As a home buyer, often the interest rate is not the number one thing where you focus. Let me give you a quick example.

Rich and Cheryl recently came to me, and when we got a chance to learn about their goals, we had them start to work with a loan officer. About two weeks into the process, the loan officer came to me. They said, "You know, based on the property type and style they are looking for, I'm not going to be the best fit for Rich and Cheryl."

As a result, what we did is to use the large network of mortgage professionals I have built in West Michigan and found the right fit for Rich and Cheryl's situation. We were able to take everything that we had given to the first mortgage officer and transferred it over to our new mortgage officer. This new individual took the ball and ran with it to close.

As a result, today, Rich and Cheryl are happy homeowners; the rest of the process went very smoothly. They were able to focus more on the important things that the mortgage officer could bring to the table. How was their customer service? What is still required to get the loan to close on time? Understanding that we have the best plan crafted and have the best type of mortgage for our situation. Believe it or not, there are many different types. The mortgage officer designed the best type of payment structure and interest rate.

What I find is very similar across the board, whether it be through a credit union, a bank or an independent mortgage person – almost all of the interest rates are the same. Where it makes the difference, though, is in that customer service; in that mortgage officer's ability to get you to the finish line, and help you be a happy homeowner.

Rich and Cheryl found there bonus material here buyers.johnricerealtor.com

CHAPTER 12:

INSURANCE

One of the questions homeowners often ask me, or those who are going to purchase a home ask me is, "What are the things that they handle before it's time to close?" Something to strongly consider is insurance. Number one, if you have a mortgage, your mortgage company is going to require that you have homeowner's insurance. That's number one.

What do you get with a homeowners policy? According to the *A Consumer's Guide to Home Insurance, from the National Association of Insurance Commissioners*; covered properties divide into four separate categories. The definitions of the property, and the extent of coverage vary by state, company and product. So it is important for the consumer to understand the definitions of the covered property. The four separate categories for your home, as defined by insurance companies, are:

1. Dwelling – The structure of the house is considered a covered property.

2. Other Structures – These are structures that are separate from the house. The connection to the house is by a fence, wire or another form of connector, but not otherwise attached to the dwelling, such as a tool shed or detached garage.

3. Personal Property – The contents of your home are your personal property. It includes furniture, appliances, and clothing. Not all personal property is covered. Items more appropriately covered under different forms of insurance may have limited or no coverage for a loss. These items include, but are not limited to, money, jewelry, and firearms.

4. Loss of Use – When a loss occurs due to a covered peril, and the dwelling becomes uninhabitable, the cost of additional living expenses is covered. Reimbursement of additional living expenses covers the cost to the insured for maintaining a normal standard of living.

Refer to http://insuranceinfo.johnricerealtor.com for more details on insurance.

A second item that you need to be aware of in this process is that it does vary whether you're purchasing a condo or a home. As was mentioned in an earlier paragraph, homeowners insurance covers the entire inside and outside of the home. A condominium policy is structured a little differently and just covers the components that the condominium association does not cover.

Often the condominium association covers everything exterior to the condo. You are going to handle insuring the inside of the condo, similar to how a renter's policy works, but with some different facets.

The condominium insurance is set up to go through and replace the interior walls, cabinetry, flooring, and fixtures, which you're not responsible for as a renter. Your policy then also covers you for personal property loss and loss of use.

So to set yourself up for success as a home purchaser, one of the things I always recommend is to interview insurance companies. The policies and what is covered is governed by the state where you live. What differs is the cost and service that you will receive.

Insurance companies come in all different shapes and sizes. Most of the larger firms, like State Farm, Allstate, and Farmers have their own agents that represent them. When meeting with agents that only represent one company, you will not get the perspective of multiple insurance companies.

A great place to consider is one of the many independent insurance brokers that are out there, who represent multiple companies. What they will do is interview you and better understand your total scenario – the cars you drive, the zip code you're looking to purchase in, and your overall situation as a home purchaser. And when they package that whole deal together for you, and you've given yourself the proper time to shop for insurance.

You know you're setting yourself up for success when you have taken the time to gather all your insurance options together. Now when you're sitting at that closing table, you know you have the right house, with the right insurance, and you're going to be able to live there happily ever after.

CHAPTER 13:

WHEN SHOULD I BUY TO MAXIMIZE MY PURCHASE?

Recently I was working with Scott and Angie, who knew that they wanted to get out of their renting situation. Scott had originally owned a home and was in a unique position where he was in an eminent domain situation, so the state came and purchased his house from him. He and Angie quickly moved into a rental and had now been there for almost four years. So, they recognized that now was the time to move on and truly capitalize on today's environment.

Well, being the educated buyers that they are, they took a look at this question, "When can I maximize my

43

purchase of a home?" When Scott and Angie analyzed the market out there – they realized that if you're going to buy an air conditioner, you do it in the winter time, right? You do it when everybody else doesn't need it. That's how you maximize your dollars in anything. Well, it's similar in real estate, in that, if you can buy in the "off" season, you have a higher likelihood of maximizing your dollars.

So, for Scott and Angie, what we discussed when they came to me was, what type of house could they look at to capitalize at this time of the year? Well, when you analyze a West Michigan market, you look at the fact that the majority of purchases happen in spring and summer. It is because the majority of the people in western Michigan are running with the school year calendar. They want to find something in late spring, and they want to be in it sometime over the summer so that they're in a new home for the following school year.

Scott and Angie decided to focus on –that market. They decided to look at houses that were in a good school district, and that would appeal to a family, but to purchase them in the "off" season, while people were still in school. Because, in theory, the houses that are on the market during this time were owned by people who must need to sell now. Otherwise, they'd be waiting until that particular buying group is at its peak, that is, spring or summer.

This strategy is proving very good for Scott and Angie. They can, at this point, find opportunities that are at least 10-15% below market value. And they're able to capitalize on being one of the few buyers looking now, versus being one of many when it comes spring or summer.

You can get additional material to maximize your purchase by going here <u>buyers.johnricerealtor.com</u>

CHAPTER 14:

WHAT AMOUNT DO I NEED FOR A DOWN PAYMENT?

Buyers, here is a good way to think about this subject and I will ask a question for you to contemplate, "What is going to make this comfortable?" Understanding the expenses that go into purchasing a house up front can help you time it so it's the most comfortable and natural thing for you to do – to transition out of renting and into your home purchase.

Now, the first thing that I want you to consider is there are still programs out there where you buy with little or zero down. And that's something to get excited about.

Let's dispel a long-standing rumor right upfront – you do not need a 20% down payment to purchase a home. With that in mind, here is a summary of some of the most common types of loans:

Conventional Loan: Typically this is a loan that fits a lot of buyers and the down payment types range for 5-20% or more down. This type of loan is offered by many lending institutions and is a very common type of loan.

FHA: An FHA loan is a load backed by the Federal Housing Administration. These loans often allow for some flexibility on credit rating and have a 3.5% require down payment.

Rural Development: This is a government loan backed by the USDA, the United States Department of Agriculture and is offered in areas that are considered "rural" – although you would be surprised by what is considered rural. Many areas of West Michigan fall into this loan area. The loan offers a zero down option that many find attractive however it also comes with household income maximums so not all qualify for this loan.

VA: The VA loan is backed by the Veteran Affairs Department and is offered to those that have served in the military as a benefit of providing their service to our great nation. This loan type offers many perks including sharp interest rates and a zero down option.

State Backed Programs: MSHDA is a program offered by the Michigan State Housing Development Authority. This is an income based program offering a zero down option. This program combines a state back loan program with the FHA program to offer lower income based purchasers an entrance into home ownership.

Portfolio Loans:

These are loans that offered direct by a lending institution that are "outside of the box" but still make sense to loan. In other words, in some cases certain properties or certain borrowers do not fit into any of the above loan types, but the lending institution is still willing to consider making a loan. These loans typically require 20% or more down (but not always) and each portfolio loan is different as it is literally a custom crafted loan. When writing an offer they are considered "conventional" loans – so the seller does not know the buyer is being considered a "special case" – which strengths the buyer's offer.

Conventional vs FHA/RD/VA/MSHDA....

Why not always choose the lowest down payment option? Several factors go into the loan numbers. Your interest rate is comprised of many factors including both your credit score and your down payment. The higher your credit score – the lower your interest rate. The more you put down as a down payment the lower your interest rate. However it is important to work with the right loan officer who will take the time to talk through with you all the right options and help you figure out the right balance. Knowing what you are looking to achieve, the length of time you plan to be in your new home, the type of property you are considering – are all factors in the best loan type for you.

To learn more about what might be the best next step for you visit: http://buyers.johnricerealtor.com

CHAPTER 15:

WHEN TO START LOOKING AND THE TIME FRAME TO EXPECT

When should I start looking, and what time frame should I expect? Buyers – I want you to think about this – ideally, you'd like to be in your new place and have time to be able to move out of your old house. If you're currently renting, and that space gets rented behind you, your landlord is going to say, "You have to be out by Saturday at noon or else you are out of time."

We want to plan appropriately. Let's jump ahead to some of the events that take place near the end of the process of buying your home. One of those items is the loan, and I highly recommend that first and foremost, you want to get pre-approved. Pre-approval is a step where you have met with a mortgage professional. Then based on some preliminary questions about income and assets and budget you receive "pre-approval" that you will qualify for XX amount of a loan. It does not mean that you have a loan, but you should qualify up to a certain loan amount. This step helps you understand what your budget will be like with the additions of a mortgage and then home expenses. That's step one.

Two, you want to think about what kind of loan you have. What kind of loan you have depends on how long it's going to take your loaning institution to have your loan ready. That means the time when the money is going to be there for the seller. Depending on the type of loan you've received approval, your closing will have to go out 30 days to 60 days from the time the seller accepts your offer. Then the loan application starts. So, you're going to want to set aside anywhere from one month to two months for this process.

Then, what I typically find is that buyers feel most comfortable allowing themselves at least a few weeks to look. Now, if you're the type of buyer who says, "I want to maximize my time. John, I want you to go out and find properties for me, call me up – I'm going to go out and see five properties and buy one of them" – that's fine. We can do that. I will take the time to do that for you.

I do find most people are comfortable with a more leisurely process. Usually, you're talking about nights and weekends, and the opportunity to take maybe 45 days to 60 days to enjoy the process of looking at a house, together. That way, you can plan appropriately, and feel comfortable about making the right decision.

And when you add all that up, you're looking at 4-6 months. That's the most comfortable time frame that I find most of my clients would prefer to set aside to maximize their real estate purchase.

Download the bonus material to start planning ahead at: buyers.johnricerealtor.com

CHAPTER 16:

HOW IS MY COUCH GOING TO FIT?

Buyers, whether your personal items fits into the new space or not, is a very small issue in the big scheme of things. Think about it. You're buying a house for hundreds of thousands of dollars. You want to make sure that that overall equation adds up, and you make a wise decision.

Is it close to your work?

Is it close to the things that you love to do?

Is it an easy commute?

Is there value in the real estate?

These are the really important decisions, and whether or not your bed or your dining room table or your couch fits into the space – those are small issues.

Why?

Because your couch, dining table or similar items can be easily replaced by hundreds of other options out there, but real estate is unique. That, after all is the thing you're focusing on when you're purchasing a home.

CHAPTER 17:

I DON'T HAVE TIME TO MAINTAIN A HOME

I don't have time to maintain a house. That's why I'm renting.

Well, this is often something that buyers are thinking about in the back of their minds. It may be the one thing that's holding them back from actually going ahead and capitalizing on the really good purchase market that we have going on right now.

Here's what I want buyers to consider: "What if you can own a property without having a ton of maintenance?" Something to consider is a condo.

The number one, fastest growing buyer group of condominiums is young professionals. Why? Because condominiums don't take the exterior maintenance that a house does. That is what I did when I made my first purchase. I thought about it, and I said, you know what? I don't want to keep throwing my money away, paying somebody else's mortgage while I'm renting; I want to own my own place. I want to build my own equity.

And I looked at condominium ownership, because what it meant was, I could pack up, and leave for two weeks, and all I had to do when I came back was dust. And if I decided not to do that, I'd just hire a cleaning lady for very little cost because my place wasn't that big. It made it simple to maintain while allowing me to have all the benefits of property ownership.

A condominium purchase is a great way to go. You can check some out on my website, http://search.johnricerealtor.com/

CHAPTER 18:

WHAT IS A SHORT SALE?

What is a short sale? And is that different than a foreclosure?

Well, a short sale is different than a foreclosure. What happens in a short sale is the mortgage balance (the amount that a seller owes on the property) is more than what the house sells for in the current market.

For example, a house might be on the market for $150,000, but the seller might owe $200,000. Now, that's a problem for the seller. Here's where you as the buyer come in. The seller needs time to be able to negotiate with the bank to forgive, or deal with that extra $50,000 they don't have. What that means for you as a buyer is that usually the seller has priced their house below market value. So, maybe that house is worth another 15% more than what its asking price is on the market. What they're going to do for you as a buyer is allow you to purchase it for less, and be able to hold onto it.

The downside is you're going to have to wait, usually 4-6 months before you can move into that house. You have to give the seller time to negotiate with the bank, and be able to wipe away that debt they still owe. So, in short (no pun intended), what it usually means for a buyer is a good deal, but you're going to wait a little longer than normal to move into your new home.

Free bonus material to help you as a buyer in today's market visit, buyers.johnricerealtor.com.

CHAPTER 19:

DOWN SIZING

Life is amazing. At each turn, it offers you something new. Now, it's time for the next chapter in your life. A point where, perhaps you're like my clients Tim and Mary, who when we first met, took a look at their life and realized life had changed drastically since they first purchased their home. They told me; they were not living the same life as in 1972 (when they moved into their current home).

Tim and Mary were at a point in their life where they wanted multiple opportunities. They may want to go away for the winter, to have very low maintenance, and preferred to have everything on one level, where it was easier to maintain. They wanted it to be easier to live.

Where we started was an understanding of this new stage in their lives and what they were looking to happen in it. Once we realized what that was, then we focused on their current house.

I helped them define the audience for their current home. Letting them know roughly what the numbers would be so that we could craft a budget, and get all the numbers in mind before we even put a sign in their yard.

What was very important to Tim and Mary may also be very important to you – making sure that a roof is always over their heads. And so, what they chose to focus on was moving into the next place first, and then selling their current home. That happened to be the perfect plan for them.

What I invite you to do is, please contact me so that we can create the best plan for you. Helping you be successful, by helping you into this next chapter. This plan can give you a very wonderful and successful start.

To learn more about downsizing visit: http://johnricerealtor.com/downsize-buyer

CHAPTER 20:

BEST IMPROVEMENT TO YOUR HOME

Sellers, I get this question a lot, and number one, it does depend on your property, and your property's price range, and how much you want to invest. You need to know this, right up front – it doesn't matter what you do to your home, most likely, you will not get back dollar for dollar what you put into it when preparing it for sale.

But, here's what you do need to consider; here are some important things that a buyer is going to be looking for, that will help you sell your home faster, and for more money.

61

Number one, you want to think about curb appeal. What is the view of your home when a potential buyer first sees it? So, you want to invest in small things like flowers, mulch, cutting the grass, placing a deck on the outside, staining the deck – making sure it looks nice and crisp. If your house is clean and presentable on the outside, buyers will often assume that what they cannot see is also in the same, impeccable order. That means your pipes don't leak, your basement is dry, your roof doesn't leak; you've kept up the house!

One of the best improvements you can do to your home is to have it professionally cleaned. Bring in "other eyes" to go through every nook and cranny – every detail of your house – and truly deep clean down to the core.

If you are considering more major renovations, those can have an impact on the sale of your home. Sometimes improvements you make will yield a higher sale price. Other times it will push your home to the top of a buyer's "short list" and, therefore, assist you in obtaining closer to asking price by setting the right atmosphere for a faster sale. Areas to focus on would be:

Inside

- Painting

- Updated Flooring

- Updated kitchen counter tops

- Updated bathrooms (such as updating showers and vanities)

Outside

- Siding choices

- Add or improve a deck or patio

- Create usable feature such as a garden area or backyard "retreat."

When it comes to the outside, features are important but we want to focus on drawing the buyer inside the home. Features that can be a benefit to the buyer and yet will not come close to returning what you invest in them are large ticket items such as sports courts, (basketball, tennis, etc.) swimming pools, or large outbuildings. These additions add appeal to your home if done well and properly maintained but they do not typically add true value in the traditional sense. If you added a $60,000 pool, your home will not be $60,000 more - it doesn't work like that with these types of improvements. Rather if you added a nice pool or great outbuilding, you are further defining your resale audience and therefore it might be more appealing to a certain buyer because of the improvements you have made. Bottom line on the big ticket items- if you are going to do them – make sure YOU enjoy them. Make sure to "get your money's worth" from their enjoyment rather than their return on the dollar.

Find other great tips to sell your home in this bonus material at <u>sellers.johnricerealtor.com</u>

CHAPTER 21:

WHAT AM I PAYING FOR?

Something I'm often asked is – "How does compensation work for a realtor?" I'd like to lift that veil for you, to be able to see how compensation works.

As a buyer, you often don't even talk about the compensation of an agent. But, as a seller, you know very well where that compensation comes into play. So, here's what happens- when a person goes to list their house, and they have an agent come in and list it for them, the agent is called the listing agent. They are there to represent the seller. During the conversation of how much should the home list for, and tips for putting the house on the market, they're also going to talk about commissions. What percentage of the sales price will go toward paying the real estate agent for their work?

It's at that point the listing agent says to the seller, "If I bring in the buyer, I'll keep the whole percentage of commissions you have agreed to pay. But, if someone else brings in the buyer - if any of the other real estate companies out there bring in a buyer – I will split this commission with whoever brings in the buyer. And that's how the buyer agents' commission gets paid.

So as a buyer, you often don't need to worry about "How much is my cost" or "How much do I need to pay my real estate agent?" It's not going to be a factor. As a buyer's agent, they are contractually obligated to work for you and your best interest as a buyer. However, you don't end up having to pay for them because of how the arrangement is in the listing agreement. Where it can become a factor is if you look at a home that is not listed by another real estate agent, who has a commission sharing agreement established. If this is the route chosen, there are many ways to be sure your agent still represents you and that the agent receives compensation for their time. These cases are rare, and each case is handled individually.

To understand more about the buying process visit:

http://buyers.johnricerealtor.com

CHAPTER 22:

DO OPEN HOUSES REALLY WORK?

Open Houses do work. I'd like to share a great example of how open houses can be of benefit to the seller. Often you're not going to have the buyer walk through the door and say, "I'm going to put an offer on this, right now, today."

A recent example occurred when I was holding a house open for Dave and Kate. They're on the outskirts of town, and what we were trying to do was maximize their exposure. One of the great ways to do that is to host an open house. A lot of independent sites on the Internet, when you host an open house, give precedence to that property; because it is held open. You get extra exposure online – extra opportunities for your potential buyer to see your property.

That said, as the flags were put out, and the doors were open, buyers started to come through. A lot of the buyers, roughly 80%, that were coming through were just "kicking tires" for example, they were neighbors, or they were just beginning their search – which was fine. Most of those people were not there to purchase the home; they just wanted to understand what the market for a home in this price range. But, let me give you the scoop on the other 20% of people that come through. A buyers' agent already represents the other 20% of people that usually come through.

In this particular case, for Dave and Kate's house, their ultimate buyer came to the open house. Another real estate agent represented them, and they let me know that another agent represented them at that time. I showed them around the house, let them enjoy the open house, experience it on their own time. It happened to be a home their agent had neglected to put on their list of homes to see. And that was one of the number one reasons they wanted to come to the open house.

So, think about it from Dave and Kate's perspective - they now had someone who has come to the house, that another agent represented, who liked their house. I made sure I contacted the other agent and said, "Just so you know, your buyers came through, and they are interested in this house. If you'd like to set up a second showing, please let me know a time and date that works for them to come through again, so you can come experience the house with them." Fast forward five days. They had come through again, and we received an offer. It was an offer that was acceptable to Dave and Kate.

Now the best part, we were able to move on to the next part of the transaction. It was helping Dave and Kate now focus on their next move, which was the purchase of their new home.

So do open houses really work? Absolutely!

The second thing that I see happens many times is when you have an open house, there is a huge marketing push. The way that I market for an open house is - it's everywhere - online, in the press, signage in the yard, everywhere. And that type of marketing push helps elevate your home, and most likely the ideal buyer will now see that this house is open, even if they can't tour it at that time. The fact that all that marketing has been done puts an extra push and draws attention to the house. It elevates the home for that buyer to see, and low and behold, you're going to see offers coming in the door.

Those are two reasons why you "really" want to have an open house.

Learn more tips like this in the free bonus material found at <u>sellers.johnricerealtor.com</u>

CHAPTER 23:

I OWE MORE ON MY HOUSE THAN IT'S WORTH

Sellers, even in today's hot market, wherever you live or right here in West Michigan, I am finding that properties are selling for more than they were in the last six to seven years. Even because of this fact, some people are still upside down (they owe more on their home than its market value). Frankly, it's one of the reasons why we have low supply.

Now, not everybody can afford to sell, but if you're in a position where you need to sell, here are two things you need to consider. Not every solution is perfect for everybody, but, let's run through scenario one - which is to consider a short sale.

In a short sale, we're going to negotiate with the bank for the difference between what your house is worth, and what you owe on your mortgage. If your house is worth $175,000, but your mortgage is $225,000, I will take my team to negotiate the difference between these figures with the bank. I take you through step by step in negotiating that difference, making sure you get out from underneath your home.

The second option is that you may want to consider leasing your property to another person. Why would you lease a property? The number one reason I find that people lease a property, besides the fact that they can't afford to pay off the difference right now, is because of their next home. The next lending institution they're going to utilize - does not want to see a short sale on their credit. If this is your situation, then you're going to want to look at leasing the property.

A potentially good audience for a lease is somebody new in town, who's just looking for something temporary until they figure out where they want to be in town. They may be the perfect match for you. And, there are companies in town, including my company, which can make leasing your property a very seamless and smooth transaction.

To understand more about your options for selling visit:

http://buyers.johnricerealtor.com

CHAPTER 24:

WHEN SHOULD I CONSIDER SELLING?

Twelve years of experience has shown me that there is a seasonal nature to the market. What I find is that when we need to sit down and talk about what your goals are? Discuss what you're looking to achieve? That is when we figure out when the best time for you to sell is.

Frankly, for some people, it's tomorrow. And for others, it's next year. So what we figure out is, how is the market going to react to your home? And then we match that with your given situation. Once those two combine – once we have a good dialog about that –

then we can determine – what's the best time for you to sell?

For every seller, it's different. For some, that decision is to do it right away. For others, it's the opportunity to learn about what the next steps will be, but then not taking the action until it's the right time in their life.

Recently, I was working with a woman, Ann. Right at the point in life when she thought she was going to be in a position to live happily ever after, retire, and enjoy life, she was facing divorce papers, instead. Her life was looking like an 180. When we originally sat down, we looked at a lot of different things. One of the considerations was, what happens if you don't sell? What happens if you just stay in the house where you currently live?

So, we started with looking at not only numbers, but also a lifestyle. There were some things that she could do to her present home to make it completely adaptable to what her life was going to be most likely like for the next ten years. But, in the end, the thing that couldn't change was the monthly payment. And without two incomes coming into the house, ultimately, the decision was to sell this house and help her get into something that was going to be a smaller monthly payment.

So, for Ann, the result was knowledge now, and action now.

Another example is Becky. Becky was in a position where she had bought a house rather recently. It was just three years ago. She thought that she and her boyfriend, at the time, were going to be in their present area for quite a while. Well, fast forward three years, and things have changed. Her boyfriend has moved out of state, and asked her to come with him. So, now it became a matter of - when is the best time to maximize her selling opportunity?

Well, in Michigan, we have a very seasonal nature to our business. Or, so it would seem at first blush. Things move fast for some people in the spring and the summer. They think about getting information now in the winter and waiting until spring or summer to buy. Well, as we analyzed the market for Becky and her immediate home, we realized something very important.

Becky was in an area where the majority of people who buy are downsizing into the neighborhood. The second type of demographic she's appealing to is the first time home buyers who are moving away from renting. In either case, they are a buyer group that does not tie its purchasing to the school year. So, waiting for spring or summer did not make sense for her, to maximize her immediate purchase price.

The flip side to that coin is - what is the potential for spring and summer? That is, how would her ideal buyer group, most likely a first time home buyer – be reacting in the spring or summer?

Well, by the time you get to summer, usually a lot of first time home buyers are out enjoying the summer activities. They're not buying houses, number one. And two, there is a high likelihood that interest rates will increase by summer, which could make her house less affordable to that group.

So, in Becky's case, it turned out that knowledge now, also turned into action now. She could go confidently in the direction she needed to go.

A third example for the best time to sell is - actually a couple Nicki and Jim – and for them, they realized that they needed to be closer to town.

Currently, they lived on the outskirts of town. For Jim, it was a good 45-minute commute every day to get to work. As we sat down and reviewed the numbers, we took a look around their house. There were a few improvements that they could do to their home right then to truly maximize the sales price when they put it on the market. One of the parts of the analysis was - how much were they going to get for their house? We looked at that figure, and what small improvements could they do to get that number up as high as possible.

The second part of the whole scenario was, they were going to be buying another house – and what does that part of the picture look like for them? As we analyzed, the next move for them, Nicki and Jim had to take a step back. They had to ask themselves, "What is best for us to do right now? Maybe our best opportunity to move is going to be 6-8 months from now when we have had the chance to save up the proper down payment on the next house."

The more we discussed it they decided to use this time to do some improvements to their current house, to maximize that sales price. They said, "When we go to sell it, we'll get top dollar for our house, and we'll have had the chance to enjoy it during that time. When we get into our next home, we'll know that we have planned appropriately, and it's going to be a comfortable move. We can enjoy being able to move during the summertime when both of our kids are going to be at the right age to enjoy that move."

Use this bonus material that I have created to help your seller experience. Find it here at sellers.johnricerealtor.com

CHAPTER 25:

NOW THAT WE HAVE A BUYER WHEN WILL WE BE CLOSING?

Sellers, here's a little secret I want you to remember. When you consider putting your home on the market, have a discussion of the entire time frame of your transition from one roof to the next roof. Do it at the very beginning.

Why?

When you have a purchase agreement in hand, you want to know the exact timing down to the minute, so you can understand how to maximize your next purchase and your next move.

The timing of your closing has many factors. Areas to consider are:

Did the buyer ask for inspections?

Are they purchasing your home for cash or with a loan?

Once the closing happens – will you be staying in the home for a few days before turning over the keys?

Whether a home is financed or purchased with cash has an effect of how fast you move to the closing. Typical time frame to expect:

Conventional Loans: About 30-45 days for most loans.

Cash: Cash deals can be fast – as fast the buyer wants, and you are willing to agree too. However, most of the time cash deals are about two weeks to close.

FHA (Federal Housing Administration Backed Loans): Typically 45 days to closing.

RD/VA (Rural Development/Veteran Administration Backed Loans): These loans both have third party oversight, so they typically are 45-60 days to close

Other factors to consider when establishing your time frame are:

Possession date: when will you be handing over the keys? The day of closing, a week after the close, 30 days or 60 days? Typically 60 days is the maximum any buyer is willing to wait to obtain the keys. Some lenders will not allow a buyer to provide possession to you longer than this (then it's considered a rental home.) It is likely you will negotiate a "rental fee" for the days you elect to remain in your home. Depending your situation, it can be to your advantage to pack up and move immediately or other times it makes sense to negotiate to remain in the house until a later date.

Typically I recommend most people plan on 30 days to closing and then however many days we negotiate before handing over the keys. In many cases, sellers need to be prepared to have their boxes packed up and ready to move within 45-60 days of agreeing to an offer.

Learn more helpful seller tips at sellers.johnricerealtor.com

CHAPTER 26:

MADDIE'S ARTWORK

"I love Maddie's artwork – don't you?"

Ok, sellers, here's truth time. The personal items in your house are important to you, but I want you to jump inside the buyer's mind with me real quick. The buyer walks through the front door and they look around the house. Here's what we need them to be able to see in their mind. They want to be able to put their pictures on the wall and their child's artwork on your refrigerator.

So what does that mean?

That means you need to take Maddie's artwork and put it in a nice drawer, somewhere else. Keep the refrigerator nice and clean. Keep the countertops clean. It's okay if you leave personal pictures out of yourself or your family. But do also know this, we're all human – buyers are probably going to look at your picture on the wall and see if they know you, or any of your family members. If you're okay with that, leave them up. If you're not, put them away. These people are invited in to buy your home, yet again, they're human, and we all can be curious at times.

These are important things for a buyer to be able to do. They want to transfer that love of the space and put their personal property right here or there. This psychological attachment is what's going to help cement that buyer to your house and get it sold.

For more seller tips: http://sellers.johnricerealtor.com

CHAPTER 27:

DO YOU THINK $500 IS A GOOD DEAL?

Do you think $500 is a good deal for this living room set?

Sellers – all right, a moment of truth – you have to listen up. It is very important to making sure that when we're sitting at the closing table, everybody's happy. And you have no idea that this is going to be this important, but here's the deal:

Don't turn your house into a giant garage sale. Don't do it!

Resist all temptation to put price tags on everything in your home that you don't want anymore. There's an outlet for that. It's called Craigslist. It's not when the buyer's touring your house.

I have seen this type of thing cloud up more deals – such as negotiating over dollars about a riding lawnmower, and its actual value when you're talking about hundreds of thousands of dollars in a house. So we're just going to take that right off the table, right away; put it on craigslist, and don't worry about it.

You can find out more helpful tips from this bonus material that I have created at sellers.johnricerealtor.com

CHAPTER 28:

I'VE NEVER SOLD BEFORE WHERE DO I START?

First time home sellers, in particular, it's a hot market out there, and you want to understand how to capitalize on it and maximize this real estate sale. So, whatever your next move is, it can be the best move ever.

Here's where you start. We're going to start a conversation inside your home. I start every single conversation about the home with a tour. I want to know what attracted "you" to the property in the beginning. That is step one.

Step two. Before I ever even set foot inside your home, I will have done hours of research on your property. I'm going to know how it sits in the marketplace, who our competition is – everything about the house, and I'll have an idea of value within about 10% before we meet.

Why is that being within 10% really important?

When it boils down to it, we have to be able to relate value to the buyer. A buyer's going to know if your property is overpriced – and the last thing we want to do is under-price your property. The other thing I'm able to pull before we even meet is potentially how long your property is going to be on the market? How long is it going to take before we have a buyer in hand? From there when can determine the length of time before we close your first sale.

CHAPTER 29:

HOW DO I GET 100%?

"John, how do I get 100% of what I'm looking for?"

Buyers, here's the deal. I've got a lot of buyers who think in their heads that they may be able to find the absolutely 100% a perfect home. But I'll tell you, the thing I get a lot of questions on is after we've seen a few properties is, can I buy this house and put it on this lot?

My answer to that is, you can. It's just really expensive.

Rather than focus on getting 100% of what you're looking for, identify the things that are most important to you. That way, when you find that house that hits on 9 out of the 10 points, you know that's an A-list property. And you know when you hit another property that doesn't have 9 out of 10 points, you can set that on the B list. That way, you can start to narrow down your properties, and be able to hone in on the homes that you know are going to be a really good fit for you. It may turn out that you decide to change the paint colors or add a fence in the back yard, or maybe pop in a window, or change out a couple of doors. It is something small in the scheme of things. Focusing on the fact that this house has the majority of the things I'm looking for is the best practice when you are looking for that next home. You will then get to enjoy what this great space quicker!

Find more buyer tips at http://buyers.johnricerealtor.com

CHAPTER 30:

WHAT SHOULD I SAY WHEN A BUYER COMES?

"What should I say when a buyer comes to tour the house?"

Sellers, here's something to consider. When a buyer comes to tour the home, we want the process to happen as it naturally should. What we want to do is create the most welcoming and inviting environment for the buyer as possible. When the buyer comes through that front door, we want them to feel as if this is their home.

The most natural way for them to do that is to allow the buyer's agent to conduct the tour. It's a great opportunity for you to be able to step out and either go for a walk or run a quick errand. You just invite that buyer to appreciate the blank canvas that's here, in your home. Allow them to start to project their things into your house, and make it their space. The ideal result of them is touring your home with their buyer's agent. At the end of the showing, they're going to go write an offer, and look to make this their new home.

We want them to feel as comfortable as possible, and enjoy the space and make it theirs.

For more seller tips visit http://sellers.johnricerealtor.com

CHAPTER 31:

WHAT SHOULD I DO WITH MY PETS?

Sellers, this question, "What should I do with my pets", needs consideration. What we are trying to do when the buyer comes through the door is make them feel as comfortable as possible. Something to consider is, the buyer, as they come in, may not have any pets. They may not like pets. Or, they may have a pet that's completely different than yours, and be a true animal lover.

What we want to do, though, is create that neutral environment for the buyer, so they can project their things and pets into your home. The best thing you can do with pets, and all the pet supplies that come with them, is take them with you. When it comes to dog dishes and things like that, find a good place in the home where they are out of the way, and just put them there during showings. It's fine when showings are over to bring them back out.

So when you're thinking about what to do with your pets, think about taking them with you. You allow the buyer to enjoy the space and feel the most comfortable that they can, in what is potentially their new home.

Free bonus material to learn as a seller go to http://sellers.johnricerealtor.com

CHAPTER 32:

CONCLUSION

Home ownership is amazing. Over the years, it has been statistically proven that the more homeowners in a community, the better off that community is. They have better schools, better home environments, etc. It is my passion in assisting others in making a better life for themselves through proper guidance when purchasing a home and real estate investment portfolio.

I sincerely hope you have enjoyed the information and stories in these pages and that this book has brought to light the right questions to ask to set yourself up for success!

Enjoy your next move and feel free to reach out to me for assistance and questions!

ABOUT THE
AUTHOR

John Rice is Principal Agent of the John Rice Real
Estate Team in West Michigan. John's passion for
helping others, combined with his love of real estate –
makes being a real estate professional a natural fit!
Since beginning his career in real estate in 2002, John
has grown to be ranked one of the top agents in West
Michigan, representing both buyers and sellers in over
eight counties in West Michigan. Ranked in the top 2%
of Berkshire Hathaway HomeServices Agents
nationwide, winning multiple national awards for sales
volume, John has accumulated years of knowledge and
experience from representing hundreds of buyers and
sellers.

The large network of buyers and sellers that John Rice
has serviced over the years has been largely built by
referral and his top rate ability to effectively market
seller's properties to the right audience. You include it
in combination with his years of non-profit service have

allowed John to positively impact the local community on many levels.

As a husband and father, John, knows the value of surrounding yourself and your family with the right environment – especially the place you want to call home. As a former wealth adviser, John's astute knowledge of how real estate fits into financial planning have assisted many in both planning and acquiring wise investments. The planning knowledge shows when and how to act on certain real estate transactions.

For the community, John gives his time and resources to support many organizations for the good of West Michigan.

When not working with clients, John enjoys time with his wife and daughter, exploring Michigan, traveling, and the amazing world we have been given!